Other titles in the UWAP Poetry series (established 2016)

Our Lady of the Fence Post by J. H. Crone

Border Security by Bruce Dawe

Melbourne Journal by Alan Loney

Star Struck by David McCooey

Dark Convicts by Judy Johnson

Rallying by Quinn Eades

Flute of Milk by Susan Fealy

A Personal History of Vision by Luke Fischer

Snake Like Charms by Amanda Joy

Charlie Twirl by Alan Gould

Afloat in Light by David Adès

Hush by Dominique Hecq

John Falzon

Dr John Falzon is a poet and advocate who lives in Canberra. He is the author of *The language of the unheard* (2012) and has had long experience in political analysis and activism. He has worked in academia, in community development and in research. He has been the Chief Executive of the St Vincent de Paul Society National Council of Australia since 2006 and a poet since 1973. He has written and spoken widely in the public arena on the structural causes of inequality in Australia. *Communists like us* is his first collection.

Poems from this collection were performed during 2016 at Canberra Slamboree at The Front and poems 5 and 6 were published in Arena Magazine in 2017.

John Falzon
**Communists
Like Us**

First published in 2017 by
UWA Publishing
Crawley, Western Australia 6009
www.uwap.uwa.edu.au

UWAP is an imprint of UWA Publishing
a division of The University of Western Australia

This book is copyright. Apart from any fair dealing
for the purpose of private study, research, criticism
or review, as permitted under the *Copyright Act 1968*,
no part may be reproduced by any process without
written permission.
Enquiries should be made to the publisher.

Copyright © John Falzon 2017
The moral right of the author has been asserted.

National Library of Australia
Cataloguing-in-Publication entry:
Falzon, John, author.
Communists like us / John Falzon.
ISBN: 9781742589411 (paperback)
Includes bibliographical references.
Poetry—Collections.
Australian poetry.

Designed by Becky Chilcott, Chil3
Typeset in Lyon Text by Lasertype
Printed by Lightning Source

*For Jacqueline,
my intimate comrade,
my love...*

The poetry is the poet
Mahmoud Darwish

The revolution is alive

What follows is a simple love story, a little fiction told in a hundred poems, a hundred little places to live large in, since, as Blaise Cendrars rightly tells us, *humanity lives in its fiction*. They are fragments of a story of love in a time of struggle. But then, when isn't it a time of struggle? And when is a story not about love? And when isn't love a fragmented but tender dialectic of *the personal as political*?

All poets are scavengers and thieves. I was given much, found what I could and shamelessly stole snatches of stories from the lives of people who love today and fight for tomorrow. The result, I suspect, is a bit like a long, uneven wooden table that sits unsteadily in an overgrown garden surrounded by undisciplined dogs, all-too-wise cats and children who caucus in the corner and then leap to their feet marching and chanting with fists clenched, laughter dripping from the corners of their smiles; a noisy, chaotic meal but also a quiet dreaming; a very simple, very human, attempt at the confluence of dust and desire.

It is life that teaches us that an injury to one is an injury to all. Life teaches us as we struggle, especially when we fail, to be more intensely, more passionately, more personally, more collectively, political. Audre Lorde reminds us: *The true focus of revolutionary change is never merely the oppressive situations we need to escape, but that piece of the oppressor which is planted deep within each of us.*

It is life that also teaches us, in the words of the Sandinistas, that *solidarity is the tenderness of the people*. Even if it is sometimes also the anger of the people and the courage of the people. In the end, as in the beginning, solidarity is simply love, because we will never achieve our own liberation while we ignore those who are in chains. Because we know vitally and viscerally that their struggle is our struggle.

This is the world in which Leila and Amilcar are intimate comrades, comrades filled with hope who are hopelessly in love; lovers for whom all reality is bursting forth with revolutionary desire. For, as Bobbi Sykes whispers knowingly to us:

The revolution is alive
while it lives within us;
beating, making our hearts warm,
our minds strong,
for we know
that justice is inevitable – like birth.

01.

In my dream I was the last Palestinian
And someone asked how many enemies I had
And I said there was only one enemy

But many liberations

In my dream
In my immediate dream
I was one of the few left who had not been extinguished
I who as Amilcar
Had never left Leila's arms
Not even when I was digging my heels in
Against our only enemy
Not even when I was dreaming the immediate dream
Not even when in the dream I was the last Palestinian

On my way to school
On my first day of school
In the gorgeous remains of Gaza.

I don't know where Amilcar came from
But he wouldn't disappear

On the contrary
He was always appearing
Out of nowhere as it were
Born of the dense night
To follow me everywhere
With his beautiful stories of Leila
Making me smile at his fortune
Which is mine

I don't know where Amilcar came from
But my eyes were wide open
Like beautiful broken structures
Or archways or the remains of history
Spying on the sea

Reminding me to learn from all who wear the chains
As well as those who work in the factory where they're made

Reminding me that revolution
Knows no envelope.

03.

In my dream I was a bad ghost
Whom nobody could see
Full of mischief and yearning
Touched by impossible hope
Even though I walked with death.

04.

I didn't really walk with death

How could I when
Because of you
My Leila
I spent nearly all my longing
In the sea

So utterly and wholly
Feeling lucky
With my lot.

05.

But Leila warns me against poetry
She's right
We are all suspicious
Because we are all so afraid
And the truth is we are all very much in danger

But show me what isn't poetry
What does not speak to the scar
What fails to say more than what is uttered
What is not sacramental
What does not make you gasp
What is not your story

Show me what is not your story
Show me what is not poetry

Leila tells me there is nothing that can be stolen

I confide that I tried to avert my eyes
And nearly lost my license

Leila you carry several hundred lonely seas of sudden love

I love it when I dive into them very far from
Where I once believed I did belong
Leila you who tell me nothing can be stolen
You who stole me from the crude enclosure
You who opened me
You who made me unafraid of the ocean
And even more prone to poetry.

I was given strict training
I was trained very strictly in how to understand

I was trained in the darkness to analyse the play of light

Leila of the Categories helped teach me
Leila of the Categories and all the outcasts taught me
Training me strictly

I was schooled in the secret courtyards
I was taught to be silent so that one day I could speak

Leila took me and we went from street to street finding stones making bread

We guarded our outskirts like loving old dogs black with love
Reeking of hard wisdom

We legislated language and rambling
Tight in our drafting
Never ever perfect or complete but with bucket-loads
Of the presence of god and by *god* we mean the people.
It's the people and only the people we mean when we say *god*

In the gorgeous guts of the day in the music of our asymmetry.

07.

Leila I have only these fragments for you

I thought I had finished my poem but
How could I finish what could not end

I fell to earth with nothing
Not even old wings to hock

Which is why I bring neither flowers nor wine
When you ask me over

Which is why I am wearing clothes that are so retro
They are not even yet considered retro

Which is why I bring nothing but longing and laughing eyes

Which is why I would like very much to make love to you

Not because I have nothing but because you are everything.

08.

You taught me how to walk
For at last
I learned
The limits
Of flying

With charcoal
You taught me to break things down
Into fragments.

09.

With you I did not yearn to be any more than I am
Just someone who learned how to read in my old man's tailor shop
Kept alive by the web of secret libraries
After Salvador Allende taught me poetry
Pick up any pen
He ordered
Write.

10.

Leila we slipped into the meetings of the people
Surrounded by love in the languages
War and the sharing of bread and questions

Anywhere

We were unprepared
But unprepared for everything

Better
You told me
To be unprepared for everything

Than ready
Only for what has been.

11.

Leila I have so much to tell you
The boy around the corner taught me the kindness of the people
Burraga Gutya taught me to turn tears into poems
Cesar Vallejo taught me to turn poems into tears
But you Leila only you
Taught me to be human.

Leila
You are poetry
In social and surprise

My comrade strenuous
And straining

And
Our daughter
Simply opening
And searching with
Her eyes.

13.

Leila

I am struggling to find a word for birth

Nothing comes close to what happens
Estrella looked me in the eye and felled me
Chan Chan ran into his moon and made me follow.

14.

One time
Leila
I told the children everything I knew
That
The Dodsons and Tomas Borge teach us forgiveness or
If you prefer
Revenge

Gramsci hope and diligence

And you chided me Leila
Why don't you tell them when they are old enough Amilcar

But Leila they were already four and two

Brecht
And here you rolled your hazel eyes
Teaches how to tell it straight
With contradictions

Nidia Diaz that when we belong to the people
We can never be alone

Darwish that faces are made of dust from stars and salt
With water
From the well
Of tenderness

Charlie Parker
To survive

Bach peace
Picasso politics

Rosa joy

Carol Hanisch that the personal is political
Marx that the political is personal

Lorca the proximity of death.

Leila you too knew the proximity of death
The red rattler I would ride to work

Long live the dirty old trains of the world and all who ride them
Long live all of us who are close to death
For this is the only way we can really be alive

My little brother died

You Leila died in the water and returned and nearly died again at least twice

One day when I am very old I will go walking in the morning of forever

Leila you will find me close to home at Pancake Rock

You are brave my Leila like poetry

Everything I had you will find in the old suitcase we used
When we performed as clowns in the children's circus

Light and lightness
Joy and joy

Remember the dirt roads I drove you on when you were carrying Estrella
Remember the bumpy ride we thought might bring your labour on
And the didg by The Sisters

Remember how Chan Chan would leave his room at night to fly dragons
And Estrella spoke with ghosts

Remember your nights in the theatre when you did not sleep

Remember how you thought yourself naive until you fell over laughing
At the naivete in me?

Leila tell me you're not laughing

Each of the three times we knew each other
Both of us slipped into somewhere else

But the last somewhere else is where we're still
Between the chemist and the bootmaker
You yelling
Baybeeeeeee to the gobsmacked world
As if I'd been lost or locked away in a lamasery
Not caring in the least what anyone was thinking

Standing me up and then seducing me
Mercilessly

This was the third time we met
And free of my good-for-nothing wings
I left the desert
Packed my things from the garage I was camped in
Little by little
And came to you Leila
With nothing in my shabby old pockets but poems and love

Leila
Everything is different for communists like us
Who find home in each other

Everything

Even love

Especially love

Especially love for the likes of thieves and communists like us.

17.

In your sleep
You asked

*Is there
A carnival*

And I said
Yes

And you said

*Can
You
Take me there?*

18.

As you were going to sleep
You asked me

Do you know any stories

Could you tell the ones
Behind us
And in front of us

Could you
Fight your way
Across the line
With them
Tell me what it's like there
When you
Come back across

Sweet harpoon in my heart

Tell me poems with blood on their fingers

You whisper

And poets with blood on our tongues.

19.

I asked you
Leila

Am I not a communist
Who sleeps

Who sleeps
With a communist

Do I not
Awake

To the sound of darkness
The scent of the rain?

Leila
This is beautiful
Wonderful

Everything
The rain
The words

Wanting to cry
When you are very
Far away

All this
Leila
Being alive

With you
Just makes me feel
I am living.

21.

Leila

You are far away

In Cuba

And I do not

Wake up

Feeling good

It was almost

Almost as if poetry had fled

And I couldn't even

Follow it!

22.

Here we are now Leila
Going about the tunnels and the drains
The oceans

Naturally the mountains
And the municipal libraries and antique shops and parks
Of the pluriverse

With nothing but the old fashioned
Kindliness
Of the
People.

23.

Amilcar gets all tangled up from time to time
And Leila berates him

Amilcar
She says

Forget about the lists
Do one thing at a time

And enjoy
Yourself

You're communist
That's all

You
Know

It's simple
Easy

Even when
It's hard.

Leila I thought perhaps that I had spent too long in the sky
And that all things turned about my falling to the earth
And into the arms of you

But I was never in the sky
I was always nothing but
Beautiful dust

I thought perhaps that I had forgotten to be human
When I've only ever been a social wolf
Or that I could not breathe when all I am is song

I became weighed down by my fruitless enquiries
Heavily burdened until I grasped and then forgot and grasped again
Never to forget again the ease

The sweet
Ache
Of happiness.

25.

Amilcar had gone into the shadows

Leila

Swearing at him

Went and dragged him out.

Leila I am young
Perhaps sixteen in love
With the libraries of the world

I go to live in one
With water and plentiful ink
That seeps from the barrels and colours everything

A library so quiet
I can even hear it breathe
So quiet I can breathe

So quiet I
Can almost
Hear my soul

And what do you come along and do Leila
What do you think you are doing
You librarian

You buccaneer
Of books
You communist of learning

Why are you leading me
Into the library's secret rooms
And rooftops

Is it just so that you can kiss me
In the folds of our poetry
Yes you tell me *yes*

*But I'm also taking you
Throwing you heartfirst
Into the places where poetry*

*Comes from and goes among the people
Not caring how it looks
To those who are not of the people.*

Leila is magical
Never does she ask me
What I have to say for myself

She knows I have poems in me
Lots of them
Good for nothing though

But she
She has magic in her
Showing up

From nowhere
Turning my nothing
Into her tenderness

Just
Like
That

Without so much as a
Thank you
Or a please.

28.

I am beginning again now
To think like a poet

With silly moons
For eyes

And a hunger
For hunger

A ridiculous love
For love

A revolutionary
Peal of laughter

A life
For Leila.

29.

Leila I know I'll only live to see today
And this is why I have spent
So much time preparing
And remembering its origins

I know I'll only live to see today Leila
But this makes little difference
To how much or how
I love you

For I love you like there is only today
I love you like I can only love you today
I love you how I can only love you
For Leila I only have today.

30.

Our children were not born yesterday
But in the throes of tomorrow

They teach us
To fly like painted birds

To ask permission
For nothing.

31.

Because of Leila
Amilcar turns the valley upside down

He goes up and down the streets shouting
Himself into trouble

Because he is happy
And not so secretly

In love
With a beautiful communist

From the salty southern tip of Europe
From the stony northern edge of Africa

From the quiet western outskirts of Palestine
From the outrageous eastern zone of Spain.

You with all that incredible beauty and you shrug it off as it were not real

I'm the great imaginer it's true but you

Leila you're unbelievable

You mess with the borders between the imagined and the believed

And you pour into me carefully worded spells and prayers while I sleep

And in the morning you pretend you know nothing

And you make me confused

You confuse me

You with all that incredible beauty

You with all that life and all that everything

All bolted down

All blown everywhere

In one great undeniable enchantment.

33.

Leila goes with Estrella to Havana

Amilcar takes Chan Chan to One Mile Dam

And underneath a tree

We learn

That stories make

The waters part and that

There's no use trying

To close

The gap

While we

Keep on

Opening the wound.

34.

Amilcar is showering
Hears thunder

It's Leila
Renovating

Leila you slipped through walls
With ease

All grace
And indiscreet destruction

Beautiful
You

Leila
Slipping through

My lovable sledgehammer
In your lovely hands.

Leila how about we settle in Sardinia where Gramsci came from

We'll live in the mountains and eat lots of beans and drink red wine

We'll grow vegetables

And we will walk with each other and fear no hegemony

Nor heft

For everything is possible

And I'll swear off the empty offerings of prose

And I'll set off each night with my hands in the ragged pockets of tomorrow

And we'll laugh till we die in our own very dear Sardinia

Of stone and belonging and the mountain hour

And the air that waits for no one to settle

And we'll love as we love

In the unpardonable ramparts of forever.

36.

Leila my face is still sore from when you slapped me
Hard because I asked you

By the water to marry me
And you did not want me

Ever
To forget.

37.

Leila reassures the people
In the streets of Tasmania

Your story is true
You told it to the wind and not to the authorities

You behind the factory
You between the fountain and the fear

The wind knows your story is the story of all who are furtive
All who bless the library

All who are discarded
Residual

Bound to win
All who are enchanted

Who find it enchanting to be alive like water
Like malt slipping down the ancient rocks

Like the cradling mountain
Like the curling lake.

38.

There are very few who know this
Only Leila

And Estrella and Chan Chan
And only a handful of comrades

I had to go into the shadows like an underground Italian
It was in the warm shadows that I learned I had a people I belonged to

This is why I had to go like a Sardinian
Full of love

Like a Sicilian
Like a hopeless poet

A homeless Palestinian
Like a Maltese agitator

Singing badly joyfully badly
Badly with exultation

With shelter from the sun with stones smoke
Kipping underneath the truck

Working on dreaming of the splendid city's architecture
Taking refuge with scallops from Tasmania

Sardines from Sicily
Swordfish from Malta

Figs from Palestine wine from Palestine
Bread from exile purple from Lebanon

People from the people
Sea from Mediterranean Sea

And stories like films made in Italy
By a bad Italian.

39.

I Amilcar
Was roaming in the
Valleys of the lost

Astonished
Crushed
Between the eyes

I thought
I was crossing the road
To buy biscuits

But
I was being called
By Leila

Leila of the Categories
Leila from the sea
Who kept my stories

Where they could easily be
Turned into anything else
With the blood on her tongue

And the
Sand between
Her pages.

40.

Leila
Did not need
A man

And she had
No idea
Why she wanted

Poor Amilcar
With his
Scruffy jeans

And ugly shirts
From
The garbage

And nothing not chocolates
Nor flowers nor wine
Just laughing eyes

She did not
For the life of her know why
She wanted him.

41.

The cards knew
Though
That

He
Would
Knock

Not that
She
Would

Have much
Trust
In them.

42.

He learned
Mind you
The art of cards and flowers
With poems on packets
Blue with gypsies
Scattered round.

43.

These are my words
As I lie
With you
At night

May you
Always know
How much
I love you

May you
Always know
My deep tenderness
For you

May you
Never forget
How I
Long for you.

44.

And these
Are your words to me
Naughty
Leila

May you
Now
Turn off
The light.

45.

And twenty-two years later
When you come home from Havana

Thank you
For coming back

Thank you
For coming back safe

Thank you
For coming back into my arms

Thank you
For letting me love you with a new love.

46.

And Leila of the Laughing Tears
Leila of the Timing

You slice
My speech with

Thank you
For making me the toastie.

47.

But you explain
That the toastie was good

And made
By my hands

And it was what
Both you and Estrella longed for.

48.

We are lying on the blanket now
I can't help asking

Where on the edge are the poems buried sweet ripe
Evasive and unreal

We're building something new
I add

I know I'm
Over-explaining

Just with the stones
From the streets here

This is where we ripped them up
To plant the little whispers of our story

Rolling gently
O'er hummus and olive oil

You tell me
Gently

Gently
Not to take my eye

Off all
The bloody

Cuts and bruises
On the beaten

Body
Of the world.

49.

Now I am back from Maputo
Uncle Joe was good and taught me

All I need to know
In his sun-filled library

Leila look I chose my weapons
To my beginner's bandolier I strapped our stars

Here in the splendid guts of the conjuncture
Is the table where we cried and told our little mortal stories

Left the crumbs of our daily crust
And our cumulative tenderness

Our communist chuckle
In the not-yet scar

The slit
In the feathery fragments

The strings in our stories
The flowers in the sleep of our songs

Your love
Oh my people

Has crumbled my heart
I go forward chanting your praises.

50.

Leila is angry she makes me
Pack Chan Chan and Estrella

Up like pillows
Lay them gently in the car

In the middle of the night we drive
For the giving of the apology

And then
She is weeping

And the invaded
Wave the healing smoke on her

The invaded
Whose children were stolen

Waving sweet smoke
Beautiful smoke

On us who were able
To lay our children gently in the car.

51.

Amilcar is all
Leila
Leila Leila on my mind
In my utterance
On my tongue
Like blood and belonging

Leila we have not
Left behind the Sea
It is bigger
It is more than our
Sweet Residua
Deep in the extraordinary blue of our mountains.

52.

Leila
For the life of me
How could I not know
That you had no idea
Where I'd been

In the forest
Just behind the garden shed
Looking for old poems
Hiding poems
Just before it starts to gently snow.

Leila even though
When we met the second time
You were a teacher

I
Always
Knew

You
Are
Incendiary

In
Flame
Me.

54.

Ah Leila I'm all over the place
Everywhere and nowhere and still
And still you are here
Loving the pluriverse so much
You fight your heart out for it
Belting the beautiful words into the
Rims of the real
Till your throat cries
That's you Leila
All over.

55.

Thinking of Leila
Amilcar goes outside
In the night

Sits on the step
Eyes the moon
Cries a little

Because he is so
In love
Because Leila has him

Heart eyes everything
Even his poetry
Even his dreams

He cannot
Does not want
To understand

The magnitude
Of
His utter happiness.

56.

Amilcar
Leila
Confronts me

On the boundary
Between brought water
And sodden land

Amilcar
Don't murder the moment
Looking for life

Leila
You taught me
To live

I will
Remember
When I die.

57.

I took my poems
The ones I made for Leila
My Leila
And nobody asked me
For anything else
For they saw all the love and the politics in each
Of my poems for Leila
My scented sentences
My satchel of joy
My simple need to sing badly
In no more than a few moments
That could be at a stretch
Mistaken for a poem
My freedom
My redolent necessity.

58.

Honestly I can't say when
Amilcar and Leila
First met up
Amilcar says it was under the hospital
Leila says outside the system
Near the school

Sometimes they both claim
Never to have met
Always to have known.

59.

I go like a poet
Into the dark
Where poems come from

Leila look
That's us in the poem
Holding all of it

Or nearly all of it
Badly
In our hot little hands.

60.

Ernesto Cardenal said *with the Revolution economics now is love*

My love you wore our revolution on your sleeve

There's you on the back of the truck with the bull-horn

Pregnant with the politics of love

And you laughing in the face of the enemy

And now you're deftly taking stories of the stolen

Through the maze of the system

Where everyone born guilty gets a stab

At doing time.

61.

Leila
Sardinia is infinite

Our intimate Cagliari
Our endless exotica

That joy
Though the sea is interior

And all that is steep
All that dances

On the tint and taint
Of the tongue.

62.

Leila told me

You will never be alone when you're a poet You'll die but only after you noticed you could live Look there goes Salvador Allende with his thick-framed glasses and his Marxist heart and his love and his steady voice on the radio and that's when you knew you could never be alone and that poetry would make demands on you and you would die and suddenly you could live

Amilcar what could we want when we are everything We've mastered the art of definition and number what with the recent memory of stone We have fire my love

This is us We set out for the ocean with nothing but forever in our pockets with nothing but fervour and the streets where we learned to be intelligent radiant with secrets that lay hidden and revealed in all the lovely garbage of our educated souls

We want nothing We've persevered with our training in the art of being everything we with our grins and our coffee in the morning regardless of the angels sent with their mute unnecessary pain

We have only eleven stars as home We have language and our rituals by the sea our library with books that can save us pull us in and take the past apart and question us our correlating water uncomplicated With nothing to ward off death

We are overjoyed desperate involved in our search for secret people who are secretly people poets who knew the art of being lost and our fumbling to find red doors that open on to the chambers of enormity.

63.

I never wait
Or watch

And now I am falling
On to the flagstones

Laughing
And looking at Leila

But not waiting for her
To lay down on the old

Stones
With me

But earnestly
Tenderly beckoning

Her
Down.

64.

Amilcar can't find Leila anywhere
She's likely in the trench or at the barricade

She said as she left the house
This morning

You don't ask nicely
For the stones

You need to build
The future with

And you don't ask permission
Of the past

To bring
It down.

Leila
Let's be happy

Shamelessly
Happy

As happy
As a new and unsure star

Or an old
Wet stone

Worn down
By the constant sea

Soaked in happiness
And happiness

Is revolutionary
There's nothing as revolutionary

As happiness
Like young dirt

Or the gesture of those
Who are deliberately crushed

And who
Because they are happy

Still
Insolently breathe.

66.

Amilcar

Is all

You know

Leila hey

The poetry is

The poet

67.

But Leila

Slays him

With

The movement is the communist

The poet is just who happens

To be around.

68.

Leila I cannot remember all the things I say I will do

But whatever you call this stream of life

It's a torrent that takes me to you.

It's been nearly thirty years
Since my brother got killed by death or something
I have no idea
Or I do

And my life I don't know why has been
Beautiful
Falling in love
With a communist woman named Leila who comes from the sea

A dark eyed
Daughter
A gentle
Son

Poetry
By the Otto-full
Enough to fill
A lip

Thirty years
Since my brother convulsed
Killed by death or something
I have no idea or I do.

70.

Estrella and Chan Chan run out of the room
While I am in the middle of my story

But I carry them both back Leila yes
Through the tunnels underneath the hospital

The base upon which all true stories
Are built.

71.

Chan Chan comes and wakes me up

I have fallen asleep with a book in my hands

Tuck me in and tell me a story

I tuck him in and I tell him a story that I may have told before

He knows all of them

He knows I have no idea what they mean

But that we both just like the sound of them

Like sailors and the sea.

72.

To be human
I tell Chan Chan and Estrella
Is to have entered into politics

You enter into politics
Just by being
Born.

Leila I have tried to pack everything
All of my six lives
Into a beautiful old brown leather poem
One that I have thrown together carelessly
From old bits and elements
I've found here or stolen there
And some concocted from everything

It's beautiful but it keeps springing open
And all six lives spill everywhere
And I make such a terrible fool of myself
Falling over spilling out

It's like when I died
Without jokes or flowers
And my poor books
I heard later
Did not know what they would do without me

All this in my hastily thrown together brown leather poem
The one I slipped into just before I died.

74.

Leila in whose arms I am crying reminds me that of all those times
We saw hopeless poets
Poets without plans without tomorrows
With no sense of the needed or the known

Poets with thick paint and pain
With fragmentary stories
Slipping into rivers at night
In the spleen of the wilting world

Hopeless poets who thought
Nothing could be ruined
That ruins were made that way
That accidents are luscious and crises stupendous

Hopeless poets
Ridiculed for their seriousness
And delicate griefs
Illegal poets laden with solidarity and bone

Red poets made of love and nothing
But the building site and sand
Oceanic at least in their special intentions
Made of longing and prayerful old salt.

75.

During the ads

I sneak the sea into the village of Leila my lover where her country is

I prise the moon from the wall of my daughter's room

And I place a soft flower in the path of my son.

76.

Leila here is the book I lent you the one you did not return
Neruda's *Memoria*
I found it beneath your pillow

I lent it to you years ago and
Giving up all hope of ever getting it back from you
I bought myself another one

For some time I did not see you
I did not know where you were or where my *memoria* were
But I hoped you were reading them and loving them

They're here now
The memories of Pablo beneath your pillow
In our bed

Now we are able to fly as if
We were born in a
Painting by Chagall

All supple with colour all light with the cumulative darkness of history
All nothing with that special lack of gravity enjoyed by those of us
Who find in the circus a constant source of deliciousness and livelihood

We who are clowns lions elephants trapeze artists jugglers
And the very very young;
We who are each of these things at once and who still get frightened

And who laugh so much that we are lifted far above the city
Where we see all the promises and reconfigured barricades
And the sky

Which tells us stories and makes us cry and lights candles
In the treasured little satchels in which we keep detritus and ephemera
As if they were Neruda's *memoria*

The memories I gave you before we began to live together
Like liquid humans
Born in a painting by Chagall.

77.

Leila and I have no country

When we fly we drop red and purple packages

Padded with the down of avenging angels

Packages with beautifully carved wooden toys

On the Territories.

For the seven years Amilcar lived in Buenos Aires
He was getting ready for Leila

And
Beside himself with joy

Nearly everything was broken
The car the kettle the future the fundament

But for seven years he put a friendly arm around his old soul's shoulder
Saying everything will be fine *che*

All will be of the well
The beautiful old one

In your Argentine grandmother's garden
The one you dreamed of often

With orange blossoms
Stone walls and the whiff of solid tenderness.

79.

Leila worked forever
In the circus in the desert

Making nets
And driving trucks

She learned to
Hear the future there

Over pool tables
Stout

Old fire
And young stars

She learned to build fire
While she laughed

In the delicate desert of
Stolen sound and sacred sand.

Now Leila I will tell you the true thing that nobody knows
There really was a tunnel underneath the hospital

In West Ham more than a tunnel
An entire world

Sometimes when no one is looking I climb down the ladder
And go there led by a devil with a torch in his hand

This is the true thing I'm telling you
The thing that nobody except you knows

Sometimes still when everyone has fallen asleep
I climb down the ladder and go underneath the hospital in West Ham.

81.

When I was twenty-three
I was taken with James Joyce
So taken that I went into Ireland
And detail incredible detail and poverty
And the poverty of philosophy and religion

My father a tailor
As everybody knows
Because the suits I wore were
The ones he made for himself when he was
Only a little older than me at that time

Fine stitching such that there were those who
Thought it out of place on my communist shoulders
With all that time I spent in the libraries
And pubs when I was twenty-three
Running smuggled poetry like fire about the Irish sun.

First my old man welcomed us
Then he launched into *Rigoletto*

Eased into stories from the war and his childhood
Poured brandy for Estrella and offered Chan Chan a cigarette

He tried to read but lost his place and brought us jokes
By the scruffs of their necks

He eventually fell over and he laughed and we kissed him
And he told us that he loved us

We helped him into bed
And he gave me his hearing aids

And we left him softly snoring
Songs from *Rigoletto*.

83.

Every year on her birthday
Amilcar would make a poem for Leila
And secretly place it in her red velvet book
That sat on the little bookshelf near the bed

It was the bookshelf Leila had in her bedroom when they first made love
And Amilcar's copy of Pablo Neruda's *Memoirs*
Was sitting there waiting for him not to take back the words
But to be taken

Into Leila
And he is taken again and again
And Leila loves him still and more
And he places poems like leaves or flowers in Leila's red velvet book

The one the bookseller said was magical
And perhaps looked like something
That had belonged to Vasco da Gama
But now was in the hands of an infidel

Every year and other times besides
The unbeliever Amilcar
Would place poems like oriental lilies or lisianthus
In the unbeliever Leila's velvet book

I cannot tell you the poems
For they lie close together
Lovely languid
In Leila's velvet vermilion book.

84.

Poetry comes
From an old factory somewhere near the soul
In that forgotten sector of the old city
Where only thieves and the foolish
And the desperate and the brave
Gather
Every day
To pray.

85.

Poets thought Che
Should not
Be trusted

Let them wander freely
If you will
But do not lose sight of them

Listen to them just as you
Would listen in the night
For the footsteps of thieves

Listen for them as
You would listen out for
Thieves or marauders

For
Poets are
Damned

They are standing in
The abandoned school
In La Higuera saying

Shoot
You coward
Shoot

You are only killing a poet
You are only
Killing the damned.

86.

I swear to you Leila
I swear I'll never be much of a poet

Mind you
I've always loved the abolition

Of the state of things
Which is why

Like you
I've been a communist forever.

87.

When lovely Will my old man dies
I sob loudly into my Leila's arms

Then I speak about
The struggle I learned from him

Old Jaunty Will
Whose calling

Like all of the People
Was to be written

In indomitable ink
Like sweet solidarity.

88.

It might be only a single grain of sand
We carry to the building site of love
The beginning of a new society

But because we are revolutionaries
Because we are many
Because no matter how often we're defeated

We're indestructible
Unlike the world that brick by brick
We are dismantling

Because ours is a love so strong
It can break open everything
And create something new.

89.

Leila you carry in you
Several hundred seas of sudden love

I love it when I dive in them
When everything is sudden

Like suddenly the moon
Turned red like blood

Or suddenly I loved you
You who carry in you

Several hundred seas
Of sudden love.

90.

We are sailors of the psalter
Made of sea

Wounded often in our salt and water
Wilfully caught in the swinging

Ordinary sailors common glorious
Come from sea.

91.

Leila and Amilcar tell Estrella and Chan Chan

Go armed with the solitude of several mournful moons and several stars

Be baptised in the name of the only thing that matters in the long run

Everything and no one missing out

In the middle of tomorrow is the opening from where we'll build today

Get used to the redistribution of life and to certain acts of uncertain poetry

And the urgency of the intimate and political

We're on the side of the crushed and the cursed

We're laden with sadness charged with hope

In the struggle is the joy

In the struggle is the red-hot heat of joy.

92.

Leila

It does not matter where we met

Does it matter

No but it matters enormously

You with your light and me with my shyness

And those first nights when we lay with each other

And those days when we stayed in bed and read to each other and fucked

Those days did not end

They have not ended

As if it could matter though where we met each other

It matters where we met each other doesn't it

It matters where we meet

It does not matter as long as it is inside our daily fire
My dreamer's lips your laughing eyes.

93.

Leila you set fire to my eyes
Since I fell for you even when I sleep
I cannot see anything except through eyes inflamed by you

And life is better than beautiful because of you

I could die tomorrow knowing that my life
Was good because of you

But I do not want to die tomorrow
Because you set fire to my eyes

I see you and seeing you I see me
Just falling for you.

94.

When Amilcar first discovered the miracle of Leila's love
He saw Leila everywhere
Wherever he was he felt Leila around him
On the train he saw Leila
When he closed his eyes he saw Leila
He felt the touch of Leila's skin he saw Leila's eyes
He smelt the scent of Leila
And tasted Leila
And even though he didn't have a mobile phone
He heard Leila's voice
Telling him that she loved him
He felt all of this so strongly
That he realised he could not be Amilcar
Without Leila

And many years later
Leila told Amilcar
As she held Amilcar
And Amilcar
Usually never lost for a word
Was wordless
And Amilcar
Who
Hard to say it
Nearly lost Leila
Felt utterly
Found and at the same time lost
In Leila's fire
That she could not be Leila
Without Amilcar.

95.

Leila's fire.

96.

There is nothing

Nothing

In the world

Nor anything Amilcar

Can ever say

That comes close

To Leila's fire

Only Amilcar can come

To Leila's fire

Explode

In Leila's absolute fire.

97.

Leila's revolutionary fire.

98.

I came from the shadows
And lay my poor music
Before you like a coastline

I left
What I always thought
Was infinite

Because
I found
The sea.

99.

You have changed all time into night and this sits well with me
Leila for I love only you
Who wears the night like a poem to forever

You have changed all time into night
And should I wonder
I who am so at home in time and unused to space

You have changed everything into night and I begin to understand
For I have longed for beginnings since the beginning
And for change even of the change

You have changed into night
And I sleep in you
Live in you
For there is only you

You are night
And there are no roads away from you
Only secret ways that lead to you
And the hour in the inner night of you.

100.

It is like the beginning
But they have been through more
And they love each other more
If that is possible
Yes that is possible

It is like the beginning
When they walked naked to the well
Thirsty in the crevice of the night
Unwilling unable to let each other go
Leila holding Amilcar tightly from behind
The two of them stumbling
On the fresh quarried stone

It is like the beginning
It is like an old story
One with which Amilcar helps Leila to sleep
While he strokes her face

He is not the last Palestinian
There can be no such thing

But they have
In a bad time been blessed
By the Yuin and the Kunja
Healed with smoke and story
Stopped in their wrong tracks by song
Taught to hold close the People
For their ground always was and always will
Belong to the People
Taught to come into the world
With the greatest respect

And with eyes blown open like Estrella
When she landed with the strength
And soul of two
And like Chan Chan
With tongue screaming *no* to the
Crushing and the cursing
And power
To the shattered and the shunned

It is like the beginning
Always the beginning

The intimate comrades

The sliver of moon

The wine red star

The tenderness...

www.ingramcontent.com/pod-product-compliance
Lightning Source LLC
Chambersburg PA
CBHW020335170426
43200CB00006B/392